Date Printed 12/29/2022

Distributed in United States by Kindle direct publishing

Written by Jerry Ayers

Dedicated to Nari Clay (mother)

Printed in the United States of America

POETIC PHILOSOPHY

Introduction

Poetic Philosophy, it was rewritten

They say poets die young, well

This is like a closed casket at my funeral

I faked my death and gone fishing

Capitalized off the lowercases

Notice the emphasis

You'll think I been here before with my predictions

This is my story, written in a poetic description

these are my thoughts that are physically living

these are my experiences, my deepest condolences

these are my fruits of labor that's forbidden

welcome to my mentality

you are here 

GOOD MORNING

Good morning,

School is in session

A beautiful morning is just a shadow of your reflection

Keep smiling, display your perfection

There's no such thing as failing

We're just learning a lesson

Life is about taking notes

But keep them guessing

SOCIAL MEDIA

A devil in disguise

A distraction to misguide

Where one can profit off the name of God

IG models, face full of lies

BBLs are exorcised instead of exercised

Wrong ambition prioritized

Nothing is really "realized"

Black women jump out of her frame

To live a ~~white lie~~

Because **us black** men give her more likes when her skin is bleached, and hair is dyed

THOUGH I SPENT A NIGHT
IN THE DEVIL'S HOTEL

I NEVER LET HIM RESIDE
IN ME

IT WAS A FANTASY THAT
BEEN A PART OF ME

BUT I NEVER ALLOWED IT
TO TURN INTO REALITY

PRAYER OF COMFORT

When your mom dies

You find yourself in a dark place

Your days used to be sunny

Now you have a lit candle for the rest of the way

That sunrise to sunset on her obituary really applies to you

Its an emotional scar that only God can expel

Demons awake inside you

There are no more happy holidays

Every Mother's Day will be a visit to the grave

Everything changes

This the time bad frequencies sprout

But you got to exercise the demons out

I've seen a bird try
to commit suicide.

He must have lost
his nest.

He stood tall in the
middle of traffic

With his wings open
and ready for death.

I DON'T KNOW

I don't know if I would have been a
house ~~nigger~~ or a field ~~nigger~~

I don't know if I would have been a runaway

But what I know now

I rather been thrown overboard than a slave

It's easy to say that would not be me

Because I'm not the one in the history books that I'm reading

I'm not on the TV screen that I'm watching

I don't know my circumstances

I wouldn't know the condition I would be in

I can only hope that I would resist

ENDURED

Amazingly, I am still alive

I have endured being crucified

I went through a holocaust of ignorance

Accepted personalities with built in fatalities

Living through the traumatic aftermath of slaves

All that time in the cotton field invested

Became time infested

IF SHE LIKES YOU

If you ask her for her number

If she likes you, she's going to give it to you

If she doesn't like you, She's in a relationship

If you ask her what's her favorite sex position

If she likes you, she'll tell you

If she doesn't like you, you're a pervert

If you stare and lick your lips at her

If she likes you, you're a freak

If she doesn't, you're a creep

TEST YOU

No matter who you are

What you do

Where live

People will always test you

Either you kind or mean

People will test you

Either you're a predator or a prey

People will test you

Either you're a bad guy or good guy

People will test you

Whether you take the test or not

Just finish with confidence

#8) LIFELESS WITHOUT MY BLACK POWER

I don't believe in going to hell for being a sinner

I'm just a **demon**strator

Life spat on me

Segregated my loves ones with death

If I turn the other cheek, I might fall in deep sleep

Life hung me by a noose

Practice of calisthenics kept me from breaking loose

Involuntary vertical human flagpole

Life tested me to the core

Knew that I was non-violent

So, it bullied me until I couldn't take no more

The heart is the strongest involuntary muscle

A solitary muscle

The brain is full of electricity, it sparks life

But lifeless without my black power

GAME OF LIFE

Life is a game

God is the designer

He forgot to debug this earth

Now we're glitches in the universe

Wrestling with my thoughts because I'm cursed

From mental collateral damage

A resurrection would be a rude awakening

Judgement day would be more frightening

than a black voter intimidation

Paragraphs full of sins

I may be sentenced to death

Paradise is my book of life

Why question God's forgiveness

When it all makes common sense

POOR BY AMERICAN STANDARDS

We had no heat in the winter

No A.C in the summer

Borrowed hot water from neighbors

Fridge empty like my stomach

Ate hot dogs with noodles

Thinking I was blessed

First day of school I wore my last year clothes

All the other kids were fresh

1 box of cereal on top of the fridge

With 1 serving left

And a half gallon of milk with one day left

I took a ride through hell

Emotional rollercoasters with no seatbelt on

90 percent of my moms mail was shut off notices

MASTURBATION

Comfort is the drug I never knew I was taking

I activated my dopamine more than a dope head with masturbation

I'm a drug addict

Self-control is the awakening

With so much clarity

Improved quality of life

Didn't realize how long I've been in the dark

I was moisturizing my sins

For a pleasure that'll last like a spark

Now emotionally scarred for life

#12) PERFECTLY IMPERFECT

Perfectly imperfect

Thoughts of her stained my mind

She left me in a state of estate

Island of waterfalls

Our vibration aligned a perfect frequency

i doubt that we inter-be

but we're individually wrapped with flesh and bone

we have a choice to act accordingly

with human limitations

I was blushing throughout the relationship

Even broke the guy code

Because she was the exception

Hey! I thought she was heaven sent

With a heavenly scent

We split because her family is whack

Funny how a puppet told me no strings attached.

HIDDEN AGENDA

Slavery never been abolished, it's been polished

AIDS, engineered by a scientist

For depopulation

Some said it was originated from pelican vaccination

Got to be careful in a careless world

My religion is no part of this world

The nicest guy in the world

But evil is the good side of me

The award of living is a death certificate

There's no peace amongst the living

You can find that in your deepest sleep

KEOM, THE BOY THAT LOVED THE GAME MORE THAN ME

I was just thinking about you today

From watching our basketball tapes

Can't believe you're gone too soon

You didn't get a chance to bloom

I failed you

Because I trained you and you still didn't make it to where you wanted to be

I should have added more basketball sessions

Maybe you would have got to the league

You earned the name Billups on the Fairmount court

Chauncey was your favorite player

You took offense when they loss

I never knew what determination was

Until I saw the fire in your eyes

I thought I had the "burning desire"

Until I felt your pick-up game vibes

Even though we didn't get paid to win

You won with pride

A single loss would have you up early to strategize

you were eager to win

destined to dominate

never took your foot off the gas

until you annihilate

I loved to entertain

But you loved the game more than me

CAN'T TURN A HOUSEWIFE INTO A SPORTS FAN

She screams "that's a foul" when a

footballer gets tackled hard

Says "touchdown" when a player dunks the ball

Yells "home run" when a QB throws a touchdown

Shouts "let's go Giants" when I pull my boxers down

Throws in the towel after the 4th round

She got jungle fever but can't play spades

She has 3 men on base but can't take none of them home

Because she's playing it safe

Philosophies

How do you measure life?

By the distance of dying

What determines right or wrong?

What if the truth is lying

God don't test us

He gave us a perception

How many directions are there in a choice?

How many vibrations are in a voice

We may hear the same sound but may perceived it to be different

So why would God punish me if this is his experience

I am just living his experience

We can't comprehend but there is something beyond living

Happiness is never fulfilled

Burning desires last longer than hell

But hell is no such place, but a concept drawn
where we wish bad people dwell

There are really no bad people, just bad
results

Bad choices, bad childhood, bad parenting,
bad luck

There are no good or bad people

Just people who are taught different

THE PRICE WASN'T WORTH IT

From a distant, she's pure gold

Up close, her heart is cold

She possessed a sound that heal broken souls

She told a lie everyday

With tears rolling down her face

She claimed a Christian path

But displayed wicked ways

I was going to ride (endured) until the wheels fall off

But I decided to drop out of the race

Queen of the mountain?

More like queen of the dammed

That captured innocent hearts when she sang

So many demons whispered in her ear

And she never ran

She became a puppet on a string

What could have been could have been great

But she allowed people speculate with their hate

HYPOS

They use God as their book cover

To tell a story of lies

They praise God every Sunday

The weekends, they're on demon time

Religion got it confused

Now God is misconstrued

Philosophies

Having more energy is not as good as having enough energy. Too much energy ruins quality sleep and insufficient quality sleep will lead to aging and other health problems. And if you have more energy than the body needs, you'll just gain weight

If you inhale polluted environment, you will exhale schizophrenic thoughts

The muscles are there, it's just waiting for you to grow it

Philosophies

The way females think, can't save the world but they do make it a better place.

Nothing more infested than a dating pool

I don't hallucinate, I face my reality because if I hallucinate then try to face reality, then I'm going to want to hallucinate

I know what type of woman I want, but there's no type of woman that I want

I understand the act of sin, but don't be the main actor of sin

CHILD SUPPORT IS NO LONGER CHILD SUPPORT

Greed is what makes them bring you to court

They want more money to pay for their cost of living

To support their fancy lifestyle

Its no longer about what the child needs

But what the mother wants

She got a new boyfriend just to taunt

Child support is no longer child support

She got a new boyfriend she wants to support

We have to be careful where we dig a hole

It might be a hoe that we're digging

Mistakenly planting a seed in a soil that's forbidden

Child support is no longer child support

She has a new expense she wants paid at your **ex**pense

Doesn't even care if you can't afford rent and end up homeless

#19 CRACKED OPEN

She can be a nun and still give a man some

She can be religious but have faith in another man

You can buy her a house and she'll sneak another man in

You can pay for her school, and she'll pay off another man debt

You can take her out to eat

But she will digest another man meal

She can claim to have the holy spirit

With low spiritual morals

She'll claim to be with you through the word of God

But with another man through the word of his mouth

Philosophies

Good guy vs bad guy.

There's really no good guy or bad guy. A "Good guy" in a woman's perspective refers to a man that follows the rules, follows directions, a yes man and a people pleaser. Doesn't know how to say no. A nice guy for no reason. A "Bad Guy" in a woman's perspective refers to a man that is masculine, deep voice, takes control of any situation, a guy that don't give a???. follow his own directions. Don't care about rules. Brave.

#20) GOD HOUR

Bodies turning into bread without the leavening
Liquid sunlight dis ease the skin
Inflated into a great depression
Permanent recessions
This how deep hell going to get
No burning sensation, just a bottomless pit
No more smiling faces, just death stares
Heads full of grey hairs
From Gods view, snowball heads
Earthlings left in great despair
Foreclosures even from millionaires
Mobful of jobless opportunists
Looking for opportunities

CURSED ISRAELITE

Cursed Israelite trapped in the states

Teary stare, sensitive portraits

Becoming shark food was a way to escape

If they aint go overboard,

Then hell is where they migrate

Western diet gave em a migraine

Fed them forbidden meat to distort their faith

Developed an uncultured mind

Made it easy for demons to cultivate

Raping slaves left an impact on my flesh

Adopting foreign language gave us a robotic mindset

Global patterns of linkage disequilibrium

Robbed of my true melanin

Philosophies

We believe what we don't know and what we do know we don't want to believe

We draw conclusions out of confusions

Just do it, but don't overdo it

The mistakes we make don't affect other people, it gives them ideas

If she had too many exes, throw her in the friendzone, because you would just be a field goal if she already had 6 guys in her endzone

I have dated a Virgo, a Capricorn, A Libra, A Sagittarius, A Leo, A Cancer and realized all women are the same

TRAINWRECK

Being a hoe locally got her no where

Now she wants to express her feelings, but no one cares

She let us jump on the train without paying a fare

Free rides was her downfall

Now she needs a repair

One day she broke down but wasn't prepared

She fell off track because she couldn't steer

Parts of her died

She fell into despair

If you chu chu

She would let you go bare

I had a season pass

I could hop on anytime of the year

I heard stories about her

Like a book fair

That means can you book her anytime of the year

But her engine broke from being worn over the years

CHANGE OF HEARTS

I've seen the devil with the most beautiful face

An angel with a wicked heart

The biggest deception ever

Left me with a broken heart

Don't got no hoes, just holes in my heart

I knew it was over once we had strange talks

We had too much in common

Except common sense

I say a word, she would finish my sentence

Never talked over me, she would listen

It was too good to be true

But she left me in past tense

I couldn't past the feeling of tense

I don't know what we had

But it was realer than fake
We were a 100% match
All we were missing a fireplace
We were the people favorite couple
We made it cool again to cuddle
Once she got paid more than me
She no longer needed my help
She left me for a millionaire
So, I became one myself

#24 WAR

Its hell on earth

Cause all I see is hell with these eyes

Heaven is just a pie in the sky

We at war

War within ourselves

Warring for the devil with God's armor

War, it's a child's game

War r us is a veteran's graveyard

Clouded mind got me raining tears

Soaked memories

Went from collecting football cards to obituaries

I AM

A war god with devil arms

Good luck with no charms

Afro Asiatic

Unapologetic

Military strategist

Biblical anthropologist

Archaeologist

Theological about my ignorance

I eat from the earth

Earthologist

Unmixed

Proud of my African descent

Human coloring blended

But the dark side remain dominant

Born in wedlock

Family still had structural damage

DECODED

John the Baptist, water god

Jesus, sun god

That's God's son

Brahman, Hindu god

Abraham, forefather

Greek astronomer

Fortune cookie teller

Shakespeare?

Astrological influences on human affairs

Modern church, a cave of robbers

The pharaoh took his kindness for weakness

Ten plagues ignored

God of love turned into God of war

Hebrew scriptures turned into Greek
philosophy

Apostles became apostasy

Lost sheep of the house of Israel

Africans Americans in America

A virgin, Gods property

Loose vagina, Satan's prophecy

Armageddon turning sinners into marching
skeletons

PRAYER

Dear Almighty,

Forgive me for my lack of faith

I've been tortured before the torture stake

Can't keep my head up cause I'm downhearted

Wish my life can be restarted

Remember me not my sins

Remember my truths not my lies

After I'm baptized, I will stumble in my thoughts

Ten times more

Because I like diamonds and rings

Anxious and disturbed by many things

If Jesus kingdom is no part of this world

So is my religion

#28 RAP BIBLIOLOGY

Pac is Jesus

His picture day was in a BMW 750

But we gone frame him driving a **Nissan 14**

X is Moses

Led the masses until that cane he was walking with turned into a snake and bit em with the poison

Jay Z is Aaron who became more conscious

Picked up where **X** left off

Didn't care about his records not decorated golden

No way this is blasphemy

This is rap bibliology

Satan the one who trying to monopolize off rap history

Outlawz was the apostles

Even though Nas was Paul, a street disciple

Rakim is Adam

Because of his wicked lyrics, our eyes were open

Eve is Eve

The first lady that made it to the top (heaven) without giving head

The Lox was lot, left badboy and never looked back

Dr. Dre is Saint Gabriel, his sound unlimited

Eazy E, King Solomon

He had easy access to the women

No way this is blasphemy

This is rap bibliology

Satan is the one trying to monopolize off black history

Loaded lux, the holy spirit

Tried to give us the **Immortal technique**

But we was **Mos def**, dumb and blind

The rainbow was the sign of the flood

Now it signifies a flood of gay parades

Before we learn **A** to **Z** we have to understand the **Talib**

BEE

Be curious as you can be

Respect other's perspectives

Be open minded but don't defile your body

Don't curse your body but rehearse your thoughts

A man can only be what he knows

Become a book

Be human, it is as close to God any specie can be

Be perfectly imperfect

Be yellow as the sun

Be black as the night

RAP/POEM

The garden state is full of garden snakes

Where the more shots you hear

The less birthday cakes they make

Forget my birthday the candles and the cake

My wishes never came true anyway

Just a flame showing my pain in a triangle shape

Church, funeral homes where kids lay

They fast forward the ghetto

But play the town that's up to date

They skip our struggle but rewind their hate

They pause at their flaws

But want to record our fate

When they can't handle the truth

They eject the tape

Sick of reality

So, I fantasize my mind

Times is hard without a table to multiply

Every plate, I divide to minus the hunger inside

DRUGGED INTO OBLIVION

Woke up in cold sweat

Vision ¼ blurry

Alive but unconscious

Numbness saturned my body

I woke up hearing the sound of life but had the taste of death

And death never tasted so good

I was hooked, I wanted more

I had an urge worse than a tobacco smoker

Indeed, I was just high

To be high is to be delusional

To be in a space that's really crowded

To see things that's aren't there

To hear things that didn't make a sound

To touch something you thought had physicality

I was drugged into oblivion

I began to refocus on reality

I zoomed out of my high

And woke up to be ashamed of my nakedness

I was clothed with a lie

Only to suffer the consequence of the naked truth

I could not look myself in the mirror

And the mirror did not reflect the image I wanted to see

I wanted to die again

Suicidal thoughts became a fantasy to me

I swallowed every pill in the medicine cabinet

I wanted to overdose but my high kept wearing off

Swiftly before I can get inside that bubble

As soon I can enjoy my "float"

Gravity showed me how human I was again

When I thought I was the strongest man in the world

I felt the weight of a cotton ball

When I thought I was God

I was the devil incarnate

I thought no one could defeat me

Yet I defeated myself

I felt happy only when I couldn't see my pain

It was blurry

My body was relaxed without a laxative

I was enlightened without meditation

Everything seems enhanced

But when the smoke cleared

I was full of distortion

I swallowed, inhaled, injected and snorted

A friendly fire to my own soul

I didn't succeed in dying a joyful death…how it all began…even with youthful eyes

I still find it difficult falling asleep

Even as a toddler, I remember anger like muscle memory

Father with post-traumatic stress disorder

And mother nervous breakdowns created a demon in me

The cost of living can determine your well-being

Without understanding, I hated my father

Without compassion, I wanted him dead

Once the potency of Mary J couldn't compensate the depression I possessed

I became possessed by Percocet

A painkiller made from Oxycodone and Acetaminophen

The opioid narcotic drug made me relax

Didn't care about the after affects

The deeper I got into my highs the more out of touch I got with the world

And when I sobered into reality, I found myself lost

Continued. It's like falling asleep in heaven
and waking up in hell

What's the point?

I prayed to God to repossess myself

Philosophies

In lower income neighborhoods

Low quality was accessible

Good quality was limited

High quality was inaccessible

Nutrition was a joke

Cheap materials may cause cancer

Man-made products were always available

When you have a good memory that you can't revisit or a bad memory that always existing, that's part of hell

Heartless, only way to keep the heart young

Selfish, only way to maintain wealth

Careless, only way to be stress fare

#32) IMPOSSIBLE

I can run 100 miles in quicksand

I can go ocean deep and do a handstand
Dig up Moses and bury him in Canaan
High five God
I will be alive when I die
Always awake in my sleep
I go to war for peace

I was deaf but heard the footsteps of Jesus
I was blind with the sight of perfection
I done seen it all
The world's fastest man couldn't walk
The wisest man doesn't talk
A snake with legs
A man with arthritis going to a crab fest
A man smoking a cig with a hole in his neck

A rat putting a human in a lab test

Seen a homeless man with a laptop

A deaf man ran from a gun shot

Dr. King listening to "Protect ya Neck"

On the balcony rooftop

The sun rained; the clouds shined

I wrote this deaf dumb and blind

I escaped death
every day of my life
I seen death run
pass me
He stopped and
looked back like he
recognize me

Philosophy

The point of being a human being is to be something. Something of value that can be treasured in the windows of God's soul. Don't be afraid to be.

Sex is like the icing on the cake. Without it the relationship loses a lot of flavor. Although some can go without the icing, but the majority can'. The bottom layer is the foundation that should stabilize all that's above it. With a weak foundation the cake will fall easily.

Reading isn't my hobby, its my responsibility because a man can only be what he knows and when you don't have enough knowledge to defend yourself, you will get offended.

MAN-UP

Man up, don't Btch down

Keep ya head up

Because God is looking down

Either we're confident or feel underground

Either we're conscious or be underground

The devil really doesn't exist

He only lives when he enters your consciousness

if you're contaminated with sin

he only lives as long as you live

eve was blindsided by blind words

Adam didn't man up, so he fell for the sacrifice

though Eve was the first woman

she became the side chick for the rest of her life

WHEN THEY BOTH LIE

She lied the truth

he told the truth with a lie on the side

when she lies it's a "white lie"

she's a good liar

he is an unprepared liar

he's a bad liar

she remembers all his lies and forget about all his truths

he forgets about all his lies

there's nothing truthful about his lies

her acting will make you believe in her lies

"I love you" **was the greatest lie ever told**

I'm not in love with you anymore was the worst truth that never been told

IF SHE REALLY LIKES YOU

If a woman likes you

She will remove all barriers

Ignore all her rules

Adjust her behavior

You'll be the exception to the rule

She will upgrade herself

She'll be as feminine as she can be

She'll be submissive

You'll be her new type

You don't have to try hard

You don't have to simp

She'll be simping to you

Things to know about me

1. I have slow learning curve, like for instance, I can't retain information unless it has sex included.

2. I only drink coffee if I smell coffee. And I like my coffee black with no sugar

3. Harmless with a killer mentality

4. If you wake up my demons, they will **demon**strate

GOD BODIED

The ultimate source of energy is the sun

Righteous conscience is my mental protein

Enoch tablets are the amino acids

Earth is round and fat

Full of carbohydrates

The study of energy in the human body is
bioenergetics

The heart, involuntary muscle

It's controlled by God's strength

I thank God for tHis maximal oxygen
consumption

I don't have 7 Oxens to consume or sacrifice

If my lungs ever go flat

God got the respiratory pump

Check my fitness assessment

No weight on my shoulders

God enlightened; faith heightened

Body fat percentage; 5 percenter

My 9-5 flexible with stability

Drunkenness is the only time you see my
postural imbalance

But nothing more stabilize than my check
balance

Heart rate; 70 beats per minute

I record my heart rate on a cassette tape

Old school, the type of radial that don't pulse

I don't go to church to get the holy spirit

Electrical currency runs through my body

To estimate the fat of my wallet

Bioelectrical impedance

I walk on water like I'm weightless

My faith got the greatest height

Therefore, you can't calculate my body mass
index

Its inaccurate

I'm static, not statistic

My kinetic chain is static

Neuromuscular efficiency on 100

I don't exorcise I exercise

You're the core and the cure

The center of gravity

You're the core that I brace

Internal tension always overcomes

External force, that's strength

Amount of stress placed on my body

Just a cute variable

Force multiplied by velocity, that's power

I exercise faith in you, lord

You kept my heart unsaturated and trans-fat free

No heart attack

#37 NASM STUDY POEM

Daily living with adequate energy and
comfort "**physical well-being**"

Self-esteem, body image, positive versus
negative feelings "**Mental Well-being**"

For used on personal relationships "**social
well-being**"

20 amino acids, 3 essential "**Leucine,
isoleucine**, and **valine**"

Millions of Gods, only 1 essential

God is alive inside

Therefore, motivated by internal drive to be
successful "**Intrinsic motivation**"

Not motivated by rewards or recognition
"**Extrinsic Motivation**"

My behavior is performed to avoid negative
feelings "**introsected regulation**"

Retrospective about my true melanin

My skull, ribcage, and vertebral column

Been involuntarily readjusted my "**Axial Skeleton**"

Deoxygenated blood to my body "**Right Ventricle**"

Sends Oxygenated blood to my body "**left Ventricle**"

Receives Deoxygenated blood from body "**right Atrium**"

Receives oxygenated blood from my lungs "**Left Atrium**"

If my blood returns to Africa, it will be Reoxygenated

If my Deoxygenated blood remains in America

My kids will be Deoxygenated

90% of Ethanol metabolized by the liver, then "intoxicated"

Alteration of memory duration surrounding a thought "Memory Imbalance"

Alteration of muscle length surrounding a joint "**muscle imbalance**"

Women: suffer from accountability and
"**Social physique Anxiety**"

We take our vitamins but still have vitamins deficiencies

What a conspiracy

The body's ability to produce, reduce and stabilizes forces in all 3 planes of motion
"**Neuromuscular efficiency**"

THE WORLD WAS BEAUTIFUL

the world was more beautiful when I was a
kid
red was just the color red
no one died over it
blue wasn't seen as pigs
it was every boy favorite color
green wasn't about money but the earth
the black crayon outlined the pictures drawn
now black is either outlined out of the picture
or outlined on the sidewalk with chalk
girls identified themselves with pink
now pink is for breast cancer
all black kids used to say they were brown
now they all claim that they're mixed

it takes courage to
continue to exist without
fortunes

unfathered through
poverty

no wealth, motherless

with your back against no
walls

just trying to not fall with
odds stacked against you

IT IS ALL A DREAM

This isn't my world, so I expect nothing
from it
I am just mapping out my destiny
I am in my own world
I'm on a planet by myself
The people I see are only thoughts
The dreams I have are only possibilities
Nothing I do matters but everything I say is a threat
Love is something you can't say or do, it's a vibration
Hate comes from insecurity about yourself
My whole existence is just a spark
Being alive doesn't mean you are living
Living is a choice….

#40) PERSECUTION AND SUFFERING

They wanted to silence me, but I had too much to say

They wanted me to take the plea bargain

But my soul doesn't come cheap

They wanted to put me under restriction

But my orders came from the one above

They wanted to take my spirit

But I was already deeply inspired

I disagreed to their agreement

I didn't have any greed to agreed

They tossed me in hell for showing oppressed people what heaven looks like

Locked in chains for unlocking brains

I've practiced humanity just to be treated like an animal

I lost my freedom in a "free" country

Life isn't fair but death ends with a fare

Prison was an involuntary vacation

My eyes darkened like I had some Hennessy

Demons always are hiding in a glass of Hennessy

"lifers" are deeply rooted to absorb any knowledge

They didn't give a F about life that they didn't have

Or a life that will never be free

My smiles became a grin

My curiosity became risks

Anger that slept inside me was awaken, and when I yawned, I sent out a bad vibration

And then I slipped in a hole

For days in the dark no water nor food

They must have thought the dark would darken my shine

But the darkness brighten my wisdom

I didn’t need a doorway for a light to shine through

The pitch blackness itself lit a candle in my mind

They decided to open the door

While I was in my deepest thoughts

They tried to blur my conscience

Every day I woke up in prison

Was another day to burn in hell

Every day that I woke up as a free man

Was just another day to smell the smoke from hell

Hell is just around the corner from heaven

FEMALE NATURE

Lie when they cry

Scorn when they're torn

Submissive when he's responsive

Feminine when he's masculine

Their heart changes accordingly

Complicates simple things

Would give you their all if you knock down their walls

MODERN WOMAN VS TRADITIONAL WOMAN

Influences: Social Media vs Grandparents

Behavior: Masculinity vs Feminine

Availability: Weekends vs Everyday

Education: Western vs Ancestric (ancestry)

Marriage term: 1 year vs Til death do us apart

Standards: Unrealistic vs reality

Attitude: Alpha Female vs Submissive

Maintenance: High vs Low

Expressions: MeanMug/Growl vSmile/Moan

BILL

I have a friend name Bill

Who previously changed his name from Carat

He's a world known businessman

To optimize his growth, he doesn't stay the same

Instead, he always changing to make himself and others satisfied

When he invests in time, he grows

When he gets greedy, he changes

When he can't afford anything

He uses his twin to help him make a purchase

When he's focus on saving,

He changes his profile (currency)

When he needs a loan

He reach out to his relatives ($5, $10, $20, $50, $100)

When he is in debt, his relatives disappear

Bill became broke because he was unreliable to change anyway

The moral of the story-is don't let anyone change you

If you want to change, change yourself because you're the only one that knows the value of your own change

JOB 12:7

Man created nothing but disease

Birds flew before planes

There were sea monsters before we became sea monsters

Mosquitos transferred blood before any doctor

Bees grew plants before a gardener

Flies, the first helicopter

Forget a car, horses have real horsepower

Caterpillars transformed before the transformers

"MY"

My mind travels wickedly

My heart is in Africa

My Soul is being determined

My love has ceased

My religion is no part of this world

My God is a part of me

My body is emotional

ALPHABETS

AlphaBets is one line bent into different
shapes

A is like 2 towers falling faCe to face

With the help of the 3rd line laying siDeways

Just to hold thE towers in place

B is a double u attached to the lowercase

C is a halF of circle

Dis seekinG to deflate

E is evolved L and F

F is a gun if you flip it sideways

G is a extended J

J is a cursive T

K is a line that means more than less

L is the firstborn of the Alphabet

M is a upside down double U

N is a lowercase l leaning on a V

O was a line now bent into a round shape

P is a half of B

Q is unexplained

R is a P with a cane

S was turning into 8 before it ran out of ink

T is a crucifying stake

U is a C rotated left

V couldn't decide to be greater or less

W is two U's

X is two lines crossed

Y

Z has no direction

FEW DROPS OF CHILDHOOD TEARS

My mom married two magicians

Both disappeared

The god she believed in, she feared

As long we had a roof over our heads

She never left in despair

#48 MOMents

So many MOMents we didn't get to capture

we have to depend on our MOMory to keep it happening

I know we aint supposed to dwell on the past

But something MOMentary I want to relive

To keep me calm like chaMOMile tea did

TWINNED

Its beyond friendship, its Twinship

We aren't sinners we're twinners

We're both short so we're twiny

We didn't have bunkbeds we had twinsets

If we were in a gang, we'll throw up twin sets

We don't dress alike but we'll never be twinless

When we get old, we'll have twinkles

We both have a sweet tooth, we love those twinkies

EXIT AFRICA, ENTER AMERICA

We were Africans abducted into slaves

For us to be freed

We had to become Americans without privileges

Hated for being God's people

They tried to subtract us

Just so they can be equal

No other race in this country gets mistreated like we do

Memorial of 5 centuries squeezed into 28 days

Like a curse meant to stay

Kidnapped and rape

Was this God's plan or the devil's display

EVERYTHING BLACK

I like my woman black

I like a black woman who thinks black

Her hair is black

Her style is black

Her attitude is black

I like my coffee black

All of my cats are black

Nothing about bad luck is black

My Jesus is black

My mind is black

A perfect picture is painted black

My poetry is black

You only hate this poem because its black

BLACK

I think black

Laid black

Mental war scars

Physical slave backs

Change my last name to erase my past

My ancestry will still be a historical fact

Freedom fighters turns into political prisoners

Goal is to be re-colonized

Freed from Eurocentric lies

You can't take me out of Africa

But I can't be de-Africanized

Stigmatized

I'm still traumatized

The residue of trauma from my ancestors

Geneticized

How can someone authorize my freedom

Continued. But not the author of my life

DEPRESSED

I'm depressed

Like peered into a pressure pipe

Waiting to bust

Depression got my stomach turning like pressed pears

And this depression is paired with stress

Very distressing

I need to be undepressed

Like sexual energies released

Out of my exhaust pipe

AS IS

You're born AS IS because of sin

Beautiful imperfections are always a win

The hot comb is like bleach to the skin

Don't be ashamed of your melanin

You put on make-up because of foolish men

You shoot up your ass only for guys to look at you from the back

VIRGIN

A virgin is God's property

Some reduce property value

Letting renters that don't pay their dues

Live freely

Loose vagina=Satan's prophecy

God betted on Eve

She chose misery

#56) HOW CAN I BE ANTISEMITIC IF I KNOW WHERE I COME FROM?

Atlantic slave trade

Sex trafficking

we are marching

while every other race laughing

from Africa, but they call us Americans

paint us as criminals

but they're negligence

born into a world of ignorance

trying to surround myself around intelligence

black history matters

~~always panther power~~

for black excellence

don't know what tribe I'm from

but I'm tribal in a sense

HEY SIRI, CAN YOU FIND HER

I need a girl that's going to love me
through all the pain
Not a chick that just want my last name
Not a chick that'll complain
Hey Siri, can you find her?
I need a girl that will have me set for life
And have sex with me for life
Not a set up chick
And not a "I don't feel like doing nothing today everyday type of chick"
Hey Siri, can you find her?
I like them with afro or braids
Low milage or just grazed

HOW DID I MESS THIS UP

She was submissive, supportive and listened

Never interrupted me when I spoke

I was pimping, then her face got me simping

exception to the rule pushed me out of my element

Never took advantage of her pretty privilege

A diamond in the rough

Never a dime a dozen

She paid me to take a day off

Whenever she wanted more time with me

She got offended when another girl play fight with me

She was my biggest cheerleader

She cheered me on she cheered me up

She was good for my heart like cheerios

#59) GOD

Who is God? You'll know who he is

by recognizing his son Jesus

Where is God? Internally and externally, above and beyond, up close and personal, and wherever you want him to be

Why is God? Ask him!

What is God? Love

How many gods? Depends on your perspective

Who made God? The human brain doesn't have the capacity to comprehend to understand

#60) DIFFERENT BODY DIFFERENT REACTION

Everybody can't take a Tylenol

Everybody don't have life insurance

Everybody can't eat seafood

Everybody can't eat peanuts

Everybody can't pop the same pill

But they want everybody to inject the same vaccine

OBLIVIOUS

Woke up in cold sweat

Visions full of collisions

Alive but unconscious

Nearly non-existing

Numb to life

Eyes opened like a casket

The aftertaste of death had an acquired taste

I was addicted

Walking around with urges

I wanted to stay in a delusional world

I wanted to be in a space

I wanted to see things the sober eyes couldn't see

I wanted to hear voices other than my thoughts

SOME ADVICE

Happiness don't come in smiles

Before the end of life

We must live our best life

Don't waste time hating

Love without emotion

Like without faith

Trust no one

Don't seek God through human behavior or you lose faith in God

Let God be God

And let humans be sinners

Don't expect more from less

Expect nothing

Promises are made to be broken

Don't be surprise

Be independent

WHAT COULD HAVE BEEN COULD HAVE BEEN GREAT

She was good to me

But bad for me

Sex was good, relationship was bad

Weed made her happy

Liquor made her more sad

Her vibe used to calm a storm

That car accident altered her dorm

I knew her days weren't long

When she started walking like she was dragging along

VITAMINS AND MINERALS (A POEM TO HELP ME REMEMBER STUFF ABOUT VITAMINS)

Carbs, Proteins, Fats = Macros

Vitamins and minerals are Micros

The sugar in milk becomes lactose

Discard the high fructose and choose fruit toast

This a dietary assessment

Of protein, carbs and fat

Riboflavin (b2) is critical in the metabolism

B12 is the largest of the B-complex vitamins

B7 is another name for Biotin

B3 is Niacin, that boost brain function

A, D, E and K; I take all my fat-soluble vitamins

Folate (b9) helps regulate carbon…to chemical reactions

Vitamin E- protect cells from oxidative damage

Vitamin K- regulate blood clotting as well as calcium metabolism

That Retinol helps with vision, bone growth, reproduction and fighting infections

I need the D (pause) I'm talking about sunlight

I want to be alkaline, but I need that ascorbic acid (vitamin C)

Without calcium, develops osteoporosis

Chromium improves insulin sensitivity and enhance macronutrient metabolism

If you want to maintain gradient balance, fluid status and cardiac rhythm

You need sodium

Concentration gradients, fluid volume, and cardiac rhythm

Potassium

For energy production, oxidative phosphorylation , glycolysis

You gone need magnesium

Selenium regenerates the antioxidants

Zinc-provides structure to the cells

JUST A POEM TO HELP ME RETAIN INFORMATION TO PREPARE ME FOR MY NUTRITION EXAM

Something like the covenant of the ark

But this is a "**Dietary Assessment**"

Mindless eating (eating without awareness of consumption) a bad investment

Stretching the intestine, that lead to **ADIPOSITY** (condition of being overweight or obese)

Thought He gave us **PALATABILITY** (the degree of pleasure or taste by food)

Even being a gluten is a sin, so watch your intake of Glucose

Or have low Glucose level (Hypo, Glycemia)

God is the **ATP** (energy, currency of life with infinite capacity)

He has the consistency of measuring life

I would never test his reliability

He's eternal with external **Validity** (the ability to generalize the results of a study)

He made man in his image but the measurements and calculations was to human characteristics, that's **BIOMETRICS**

All religions have a **systematic review** (a review where scientists systematically gather all research on a topic and evaluate it based on predefined criteria and rules)

But God is the only scientist

(building blocks of proteins) Amino Acids

The devil is the uncontrolled variable with a **HYPOTHESIS** (Set of observations)

His goal is to predict a outcome from a bet he made with the master scientist

But God gave us the **META-ANALYSIS** (a statistical analysis of a group of studies to access the overall weight of the problem)=bible study

Now the bible has been translated to **GMO**s (genetically Modified Organisms)

We spray chemicals on our plants to distort the **POLYPHENOLS** (class of natural chemicals found in plants that have unique biological effects when consumed)

The most cost of death is a heart attack

We **HYDROGENERATE** till our heart collapse (the process of forcing hydrogen into vegetable oil to create a semi-solid saturated fat

Translation: **Trans-fat** (artificially fatty acids occurs when hydrogen is added to liquid vegetable oils

To not to be (prone to oxidated damage) unsaturated fatty acids

We need **self-EFFICACY** (a person's confidence that the can successfully execute behaviors required to produce outcome)

Or death would be claimed by **fatty acids**

(organic compounds with long carbon chains that are saturated or unsaturated)

Thoughts of a master scientist

LIPOLYSIS (breaking triglycerides into free fatty acids)

HYDROLISIS (breakdown of one large molecule into smaller molecules)

In a cold world, we need **HEMGLOBLIN** (an iron containing protein found on red blood cells, binds oxygen and other molecules for transport of the blood)

We like a oxen without oxygen

We're weak without **collagen** (a protein formed of a triple helix structure with great tensile strength found in the skin, muscles, connective tissue and bone)

And softer than **Keratin** (a protein found in hair and nails)

So we need baptism to dissolve our sins in water

No need to be **HYPROPHOBE** (water fearing, will not dissolve in water)

Ketones is like negative energy (group of incompletely metabolized fat fragments

That are normally produced during fat metabolism in the absence of adequate carbs

Instead, we need to be **catabolic** (breakdown of nutrients to release energy)

Then we would be able to get a good night sleep

With a good **resting metabolic rate** (amount of energy an individual uses at rest in order to sustain basic processes in the body)

Philosophies

It isn't a small world, its big enough for people to walk out of your life

Nobody carries more trauma than a black woman

A cellular device can have your mind traveling through bad frequencies

Rule number one, plan A never works, always focus on plan B

DON'T LOSE YOU

Its easy to lose **you**rself in a soul less world

And become multiple scattered personalities trying to host one body

When the mind is gone, there's no longer **you**

What makes you **you** is covered in fog

All it takes is one pill to slip

One way trip to the nose is hell's meal ticket

A hidden ingredient wrapped in the blunt

Then you inhale a ghost

You become cold

Because you exhaled **you**

It'll take a lot of good memories to bring **you** back

INTER-BE

If we don't inter Be

Then outer existence we be

If we are what we eat

Then we'll be arti**fish**al human beings

The ocean that was once plenty is now empty

The clouds that was once clouds is now toxicity

Taxpaying our way to famine

8 billion but we're a endangered specie

If we don't rid our ego out our system

We will ruin the ecosystem

Religion will be followed

Once the word of god loses its value

We try manipulating nature

But Nature will reverse back to nature

Mother earth will put on a new make-up

NOTHING SURPRISES ME ANYMORE

hell in heaven

cancer hosting an alkaline body

structural damage in a wedlock family

teardrops and closed caskets

Cursed seed equals light skin

We fish for Frankinfish

10 million members but can't find a real
person on plenty of fish

Science is the new religion

Obesity is normalized and healthy

Standard of beauty is a BBL model on IG

DEDICATED

She was born in 1956

Died at 59 on June 12th

I was 32 when I first experience hell

Her birthday was June **20**th,

8 more days she would have been **60**

Life cut short and death extended long

I new her time was running out when she started dragging along

Her lifeforce expelled at 581 Madison Ave

Pre-spawned at section **48**, **37** is the grave

for 7 days, lot **28** is where her lifeless body remains

Since then, I have never been the same

YOU HAVE REACHED THE END OF THIS BOOK

Upon completion, you have read 0000000.1 percent of my mind

You've gained a handful of new perspectives

You've traveled through my flightless thoughts

I gave you a glimpse of what I saw

You swam deep through the depths of my conscience and learned my behavior

And treasured your own ignorance to shore

You know that I like my coffee black with no sugar and only drink coffee if I smell it

You know that I'm a personal trainer and poeticized my study guide in order to remember it

Thank you for listening, thank you for understanding even if you find it incomprehensible

This is my Poetic Philosophy

www.ingramcontent.com/pod-product-compliance
Lightning Source LLC
LaVergne TN
LVHW010356160826
845677LV00005BA/1291
* 9 7 9 8 3 7 1 6 8 7 2 1 0 *